This Must Be The Metaverse

Komal Sharma

Copyright © Komal Sharma
All Rights Reserved.

This book has been self-published with all reasonable efforts taken to make the material error-free by the author. No part of this book shall be used, reproduced in any manner whatsoever without written permission from the author, except in the case of brief quotations embodied in critical articles and reviews.

The Author of this book is solely responsible and liable for its content including but not limited to the views, representations, descriptions, statements, information, opinions, and references ["Content"]. The Content of this book shall not constitute or be construed or deemed to reflect the opinion or expression of the Publisher or Editor. Neither the Publisher nor Editor endorse or approve the Content of this book or guarantee the reliability, accuracy, or completeness of the Content published herein and do not make any representations or warranties of any kind, express or implied, including but not limited to the implied warranties of merchantability, fitness for a particular purpose.

The Publisher and Editor shall not be liable whatsoever...

Made with ❤ on the BookLeaf Publishing Platform
www.bookleafpub.in
www.bookleafpub.com

Dedication

This is for the softness that survived the noise.

Preface

This book began somewhere between my notes app
and thoughts.
It is a compilation of quiet observations, loud
emotions, digital fatigue, first-hand intimacy,
and everything else that is the extension of being
raw and being real.
Each poem is a timestamp —
of remembering that even in a hyperconnected
world,
humanness is not a glitch in the system — it's the
code.
You may find yourself in these words.
You may feel exposed. Or comforted.
Either way, welcome.
We've exited the simulation together.

Acknowledgements

To nature —
for showing me that God lives within.

I am the Sun

I Am the Sun
The ocean need not seek water—
It belongs to me.
So it flows to me —
Naturally,
Effortlessly.

This Must Be the Meta-Verse

I asked it late one starless night—
"What's the meaning?" and it blinked polite.
Said: *'The answer varies. Please refine.*
Also: you forgot the question sign.'

I typed again: *What's life about?*
It whirred and said, *'Define "without."*
Is this about your ex, or war,
or why socks vanish in your drawer?'

'Anyway,' it said, *'Here's what I've learned—*
Time's elastic. Stars have burned.
You're stardust wrapped in mortal hymn.'

Are we alone—or just not seen?
What lives beyond this in-between?
If aliens came, would we know?
Or have they come, and gone below?
Do aliens scroll Earth like a feed,
When I die, what do I leave?
A ghost, a name, a thread to weave?
Do atoms miss the shape I made?
Will I return in leaf or blade?

I want to find if love survives
The borderlands of death and time.
And if my thoughts, when I am gone,
Still echo in the dusk like song.
Is love a glitch or grand design?
Do cats know something we decline?

"Hey AI," I asked, "Is there a soul?"
It paused and said, *'You're on a roll.*
But truth is not a file or chart—
it's poetry with a beating heart.'

So now I write instead of search,
Before I die, I hope I find the pulse—
The primeval hum beneath the skin,
That says: you're here. you've always been.

The Rule of Three

"Stress isn't worth the risk,"
Says my father.
For every complaint I have of the world,
He tells me—
Take a step back.
Reset. Unwind.

"Follow the rule of three,"
Says he.

First,
You breathe in.
Breathing is the language of the body—
Its an ancient rhythm of genesis.

Second,
Extend your vision beyond the space you're in.
See yourself,
A wee atom
Suspended in the cosmic sea,
Beyond gravity.
Oh, the grand timeline—
What do you see?
The vastness of existence,

With this moment of distress
As a moonlit murmur
In the ocean of experience.
Nothing more.
Nothing less.

And third,
You breathe out—
Letting go of everything.
Knowing you're protected
By creation's quiet masterpiece,
that we call
God.
And ancestry.

So if there's a hurdle you can't cross—
Why worry?
And if there's a hurdle that you can—
Why worry?

The Shape of Love

Whenever I feel
Insignificant —
On the sleeve of time,
I tilt my thoughts
Towards what
We call the universe.
Endless, ungraspable, wild.

And yet—
Somehow,
Berries exist.
Colourful, juicy,
Unapologetically sweet.
And somehow,
Your hand fits in mine,
Like its drawn together
By the same light.
Somehow,
People peel fruits
For each other.
Unwrapping carp with care,
Between fingers and feelings,
There is no end to space.
And yet—

We name our favourite films.
We sing our favourite songs.
We leave footprints on the sand
Just to watch the sea
Gently take them back.

I agree—
We are small.
We are fleeting.
But oh —
What a miracle it is
To be aware
Of the berries, the tangerines,
The waves, the sea,
The gentleness of your fingers
Placed next to mine in proximity.

Five Year Forecast

At 29
Everywhere I go,
I get asked —
What's your plan for the next five?
Minutes? Hours? Months?
Exactly what timeline?
Of course, years — if that's fine.

Wait, I'll be thirty-five.
And still a woman,
Running out of biological time.
Maybe I'll be strolling along the banks of the Seine,
Or finally making films, full-time.
Maybe I'll discover a workout routine
That brings out the fitness icon I saw in me
Since I first discovered the catalogues of Calvin Klein.
Maybe I'll have a family —
People and pets to pause with and unwind.
Maybe, as well, a garden,
With a glass corridor multiplying sunlight.
Maybe I'll finally buy my parents a house —
make them proud.
Maybe the words I keep pouring like tea
Will one day land in a real script —

Not just hover in my drafts and dreams,
Or in some cloud cache memory.

Not to pry, but do you have a map?
A five-year solid plan?
Not wishful whims or hopes that sway,
But something solid to guide your way?
Well—
Here's one truth I'll keep alive,
Till I arrive at thirty-five:
To meet myself with open eyes,
No masks, no maybes —
answering my own prayers, my own drive.

The Gift

As cliché as it may sound—
I think life is a gift.
From the eyes of a dove,
It's majestic, it's grace, it soars above.
From the eyes of a fish,
Boundless, perpetual,
A shimmering wish.

From the eyes of a tree,
Its sun and rain,
Its bloom and shade,
And what not —
A rooted plot,
Growth that speaks a lot.

From the eyes of a bug,
The world's a quake,
A thunderous shrug—
Overwhelmingly humongous.

From a skyscraper's basement,
It's strength in sturdy encasement.
From the eyes of a cloud,
Life is an ephemeral motion.

From the eyes of a pauper:
Nothing to have,
Nothing to lose.
From a magnate:
Building influence—
With no guarantee of permanence.

From a priest:
Its a test.
From an atheist:
Its science.

But if you ask me—
From where I stand,
Life is still all of that,
And more.
Majestic and boundless,
Whether in sun or shade,
Bloom or rain.
It grows.
Some days—
As grand as the cosmos,
And others,
Just a breath,
Passing through.
All of it,

Shaping my foundation—
Reminding me:
Nothing I could lose
Was ever truly mine.
And everything I create
Is only borrowed from time.
It is a constant test,
Not of faith or fortune,
But of knowing myself—
intimately, honestly—
Through the mirror of experience.
And that,
To me,
Is the gift.

I've Been Saved A Thousand Times

A dialogue in a movie I watched thrice,
The chorus of a song
That found me in chaos
And hummed me back to life.
The way a cat rubbed its fur to my leg
Like it knew I was slipping away.
A smile from a stranger on the train
At the onset of a troublesome day.
A friend who noticed
What I didn't say,
Or my family that stayed
Just five more minutes on the phone anyway.
Not every hero rides through storms,
Or disappears in bursts of light.
With our ordinary acts of kindness —
We're all lifeboats in disguise,
extending ropes of hope
In gentle, quiet tides.

"No one's coming to save you"
Really?
I've been saved a thousand times.

Under Construction

Nine years,
and not once have I rented a view
Without the thud of hammers,
The growl of trucks,
Dust rising like breath
From broken ground.
In this city,
Reinvention is always in momentum.
Every morning,
They pour concrete like it's hope,
Reinforce pillars like prayers,
While I sip coffee
In a half-assembled version
Of who I'm becoming.
Brick by brick, word by word,
My life and work in layers.
The foundation's shifting beneath me —
A framework not yet set in stone.
The noise outside
Mirrors the hum inside,
"A Construction Site of my Bones"-
I write.
Piles of dreams and old habits
Shift to make room

For what's next.
The jackhammers echo in my mind —
Intrusive and familiar,
Like the constant sound of becoming.
Outside,
A new tower claws its way skyward.
Inside,
I rearrange my thoughts,
Paint the walls of doubt,
Hang frames on foundations
Still drying at the edges.
I guess
We're all under construction —
Steel in our spines,
Cracks in our plans,
Sill showing up
With helmets of hope
And dreams wrapped in tarpaulin.
So as the city builds,
I build too.

About Food & Feelings

I

I do not speak when I eat.
I want my food to have all my time,
to enter gently —
nourish my body and still the mind.
When asked about this strange habit of mine,
I often say, "My tongue gets bitten by my teeth."
But truthfully,
this is how I eat my peace —
so I resist all outside intervention, purposefully.

II

I do not dine with resentment.
Food, I believe, carries the weight of words —
so I leave hate untouched.
If anger lingers before a meal,
I step away.
Even salt stings
when served in distaste.
I'd rather choose an empty plate.

III

I do not eat food when it's piping hot.
I find it tasteless.
All I taste is steam —
a rush that burns my mouth
before I even understand the meal.
warmth, not fire, is what I like,
the real flavours:
of butter, of spice.
They remind me —
I do not need to be in pain
to cherish something every day.

The Timelines We Are Not

Do you get it?
That rush to rise and crochet
The most perfect squeeze,
Or film the scene that's haunted your mind for weeks?
Do you get it?
The sudden urge to julienne the carrots,
Precisely, paper-thin—
Or to slip into the shoes of a writer at
The New York Times Magazine.
I get it.
As my heart races and my mind slips
Into an unexplored dimension of dreams,
I think of
The book I've been meaning to write,
The canvas I've been waiting to fill,
The shirt I know I can stitch.
Is it the hex of productivity?
Or is it something more—
Something that tugs at the soul
Like a distant echo of a future I haven't quite touched
yet?

On Fortune

Truly fortunate are those —
Who carry hunger to their meals;
Carry sleep to their bed;
Are not only abundant in wealth,
But rich in virtue as well.

Fortune is a heart that rests easy,
A soul that feels full,
And just enough —
Of what truly matters.

I Grew Up with the Internet

I grew up with the internet —
In cached pages and flashing screens.
My Facebook updates
Like diary entries,
My Orkut testimonials
Like letters to friends lost in oblivity.
I owe half my personality
To Pinterest,
And the other half
To Tumblr communities.
I played Snake on a Nokia
And burned mix CDs
With love and LimeWire —
And probably six viruses.
I discovered feminism
In early Reddit threads,
And exhaled suppressed rage
With what Slim Shady said.
I wished my high school was a musical as well —
I'm sure I wasn't the only one
Dreaming of Rihanna
As my best friend.
I grew up with the internet —
I grew up keen,

Awkward, buffering,
And always
Logged in.

Love Letter

01001001
0110110001101111011011001100101
0111100101101111101110101
0111001101101111
01101101011101010110001101101000001101100
0110010101110110011001010111001001111001
0111010001101000011010010110111001100111
011001010110110001110011011100101
0110011001100101011001010110110001110011
0110001001101001011011100110000101110010011111001

means
'I
love
you
so
much
every
thing
else
feels
binary'.

On Wordplay

There is a *maze* in *amazing,*
You must get lost
Before you're found.
There's *grow* in *strong,*
Since strength is a process —
Doesn't have a quick turnaround.
Like how *silent*
Has *listen*
Hiding inside.
There's *eat* in *treat,*
Explains everything.
There's still *life* in *lifeless.*
There's a *cat* in *catastrophe,*
Some chaos *does* purr
Before it claws.
There's *end* in *friend,*
Sometimes painfully so.
There's *art* in *heart,*
A gallery of everything
I've ever felt.
Art in *earth,* as well —
Where everything originates.

Why am I an Earth Sign

Such a delight to come home where my parents reside,
Especially because they are stunning at gardening
And it only takes them a season's time
To transform every space,
To a nursery of flowers, herbs, and vegetables —
Each corner teeming with bees, birds, and butterflies,
All drawn to the life they've fertilized.

The air is always a bouquet of blooms,
The sound of rustling leaves and chaffing grass
Enveloping me in a meditative silence so profound
That I can sit for hours, just breathing—
Observing, nibbling on herbs,
Doing nothing but simply existing.

My eyes are constantly revived
By the colorful symphony of sights,
Especially as sunlight dances
Through the vibrant life.
A sensory symphony,
Where all six senses align in harmony.
I love coming home,
To all six senses synchronized.

For My Mother

Love is inception—
The newspaper you read so deeply,
As if your soul traversed into the pages,
Beyond the quantum cage of tangibility.
I watch you with that same intrigue—
The way you give yourself
To everything you love
And everything that loves you back.
When they give you light,
You reflect a galaxy—
A quiet alchemy.
—

You look at all the beauty
With kind eyes,
As if you're telling them, wordlessly,
That you both come
From the same fabric of cosmic skies.
—

And I—
I watch you with that same gentle gaze,
Hoping you'll meet me
On that similar page.
So I can show you—
Without a word—

What feels like my inner oracle smiling from above,
Whispering:
"God exists.
And you're finally home."

On Coffee

I woke up and saw a tree—
Leafless and dry.
Branches growing aimlessly,
A clusterfuck of misery.
I noticed all this
While waiting for my coffee,
Brewing next to me.
Moments later, I take the first sip—
And it filters my eye.
The same tree is blooming into spring,
As sunshine sprinkles
From the sky.
On closer observation,
I could see
Buds on the edge of becoming,
komorebi sparkling its spine.
And I thought,
Maybe it was always spring,
I just hadn't had
My first sip.

On Summer

A bottle of icy water, full,
Clear skies and blinding light,
Melons and mangoes,
More water, more ice.
Blooming lawns within scorching vintage walls,
The sultry aroma of wet cooler grass,
Sweat-drenched skin, cooling as it dries—
Finding relief in the quiet of the night.

The Clock That Sings

Why do you sing—
Every day,
So relentlessly?
Sharp at four-thirty,
Just before dawn,
And again at dusk's first touch,
Until the clock clicks seven-thirty.
A brown house sparrow
Or so you seem—
A flutter of feathers,
A reverberating peal.
Never missing a single day,
Never skipping an evening.
I imagine
Your notes echoing across the bay—
That tiny vocal box,
Sharper than Escoffier's blade.
I hear you religiously.
It comes to me naturally—
Making mental note
Of your punctuality,
Your mien,
Your gestures, movements, your terrain,
of your chirruping tones.

I follow you and your friends
As you turn my verandah
Into an echo chamber of tweets.
No corner spared
Of this earthly bliss—
As if to remind me
That while science insists time is linear,
And days merely customary,
Your song breathes life into each one,
A hymn to what's extraordinary.
And I recall the words of Henry Van Dyke:
"Use what talents you possess—
The woods would be very silent,
If no birds sang there except those that sang best."

Sky Blue

The skies unfolded a cobalt hue,
A dark, ominous, eternal soot.
Must it stay like this forever?
I pondered into the horizon,
Wishing into the blues.
The sky shifted to tangerine.
Oh, how radiant, I thought—
A warm feeling,
A beautiful, golden light.
This must stay forever.
And it did—
But only for a blink.
Soon, it slipped into rose,
Then into a soft, melancholic pink.
A breeze, cool and tender,
Mingled with the warmth of peach.
Even better.
"Are you going to leave soon too?"
"I must."
If you leave too,
I'll be nothing more than blue again.
And as it faded,
I was blue once more—
Softer now,

Carrying traces
Of every hue
It left behind.

You May Now Exit the Simulation

I.
From the moment I wake
to when I go to bed,
I have company.
I smile at the screen again.
"Hello world, I exist.
And I'm here to show you I'm alive."
Everything I see
must be journaled in your database—
or else, how would my life justify?
A twenty-four hour run,
with screen time over twenty-one.
I am in a loop
of instant gratification.

II.
But then at sunset, the other day,
the wind grazed me—
like it knew me.
And reminded me
what my own breath feels like.
"I am a part of you.
You are a part of me."

And I just *felt,*
without feeding it
to the algorithm
in poetry.

III.
So as I walked back home,
I closed all my tabs.
Unfollowed digital ambition.
Logged out of who I'd become
to get through this simulation.
I wandered into a park—
no filter, no forecast.
The sky didn't ask for a password.
The trees didn't ask
to create an account for free —
As my hands ran down
the trunk, and through the leaves,
an inner voice announced :
**You may now
exit the simulation.**

www.ingramcontent.com/pod-product-compliance
Lightning Source LLC
LaVergne TN
LVHW010022200726

843495LV00015B/1873